THE HOW, WHAT & WHY OF MAMMALS

D0182994

GARETH COLEMAN

Heinemann Educational Publishers
Halley Court, Jordan Hill, Oxford OX2 8EJ
a division of Reed Educational & Professional Publishing Limited

Heinemann is a registered trademark of Reed Educational & Professional Publishing Limited

OXFORD   MELBOURNE   AUCKLAND
JOHANNESBURG   BLANTYRE   GABORONE
IBADAN   PORTSMOUTH (NH) USA   CHICAGO

First published 1999

03 02 01 00 99
10 9 8 7 6 5 4 3 2

British Library Cataloguing in Publication Data
A catalogue record for this book is available from the British Library.

ISBN 0 435 09673 7   *The How, What and Why of Mammals* single copy

ISBN 0 435 09674 5   *The How, What and Why of Mammals* 6 copy pack

Illustrations: John Butler/Ian Fleming Associates, page 4. Ed Stuart, pages 5, 15, 16, 20,
22, 23, 24 top. Mike Atkinson/Garden Studio, pages 6 top, 7 top, 8, 12-13, 14. Doreen
McGuinness/Garden Studio, contents top right, bottom right, pages 6-7 bottom, 10 top, 27, 30,
bottom left. Miranda Gray/Maggie Mundy, contents top left, pages 10 bottom, 11 top, 24
bottom, 25, 28, 29. Steve Weston/Linden Artists, pages 18-19.

Photos: Andy Rouse, page 9 top. Stuart MacFarlane, page 9 bottom. Professor P M Motta, G
Macchiarelli, S A Nottola/Science Photo Library, page 17. Heather Angel, page 21. Andrew J
Purcell/Bruce Coleman Ltd, page 26. Jane Burton/Bruce Coleman Ltd, page 29.

Designed by Traffika Publishing Limited
Printed and bound in the UK

Contents

What are **mammals?**

Mammals are a group of animals that share certain characteristics. There are about 4000 different species of mammals in the world. Many different types of animals are classified as mammals, from the biggest whale to the tiniest mouse. So what do all these animals have in common?

Mammal features

Firstly, all mammals are warm-blooded. Their bodies stay at a constant temperature, however hot or cold their surroundings are. This means that they can stay active even when it is very cold.

Secondly, mammals have hair. Hair comes in many different forms, including fur, wool, whiskers, spines, prickles and even some types of horns. This hair keeps out the cold, wind and rain, and so helps the animal to stay warm.

Finally, all mammals feed their young on their mother's milk. Mammals also usually look after their young for longer than other animals.

a skeleton

external ears

lungs

a heart

four limbs

'warm blood'

a large, well-developed brain

eyesight that adapts to its surroundings

a sensitive nose and mouth

hairy or furry skin

milk glands for suckling its young

young that are born live, not hatched from an egg

How long have mammals been on Earth?

Mammals are the most recent development in the evolutionary chain. As far as we know, they first appeared about 200 million years ago. At that time, the Earth was dominated by huge dinosaurs and reptiles. The first mammals were probably small, shrew-like creatures that survived by eating insects and stealing dinosaur eggs. After the dinosaurs died out, about 65 million years ago, mammals quickly evolved to take their place as the dominant group.

The evolution of life.

3,500 million years ago
– bacteria and algae

600 million years ago
– jellyfish and sea worms

500 million years ago
– jawless fish

420 million years ago
– land plants and insects

400 million years ago
– amphibians

350 million years ago
– reptiles

210 million years ago
– dinosaurs

200 million years ago
– early mammals

150 million years ago
– birds

100 million years ago
– flowering plants

65 million years ago
– dinosaurs die out

50 million years ago
– bats and whales

40 million years ago
– monkeys and horses

20 million years ago
– seals

2 million years ago
– humans

What is a skeleton?

A skeleton is a collection of bones, joined together to enable an animal to stay upright and move around. All mammals have an internal skeleton which is made up of a skull, a backbone, a rib cage, hip bones and limbs.

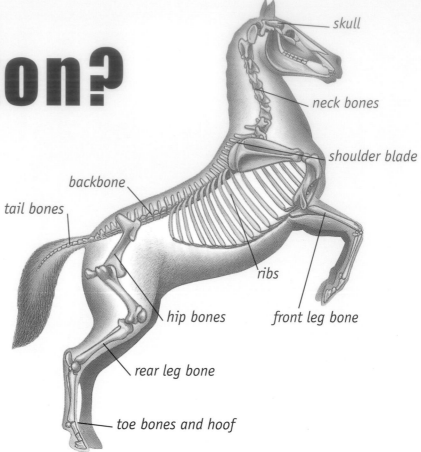

skull

neck bones

shoulder blade

backbone

tail bones

ribs

hip bones

front leg bone

rear leg bone

toe bones and hoof

Name the skeleton

Mammals' skeletons have evolved in different ways to match the needs of different animals. Horses, for example, have long, slim leg bones so that they can run quickly. Giraffes have very long neck bones so that they can reach to eat the leaves on tall trees. Can you work out which mammals these skeletons belong to?

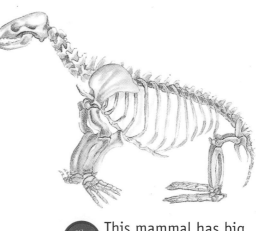

(See page 30 for answers)

1 This mammal has big shoulders and strong front legs to help it to swim in rough seas.

How many bones do humans have?

An adult has about 206 bones in their skeleton. Nearly half of them are in the hands and feet. A newborn baby has over 800 bones. This makes its body more flexible, so that it can be born more easily. As the baby grows, many of the bones, such as those in the skull, join together.

Why are humans' legs much longer than their arms?

Humans are the only mammals who spend most of their time walking on two feet. This has led to our leg bones becoming much longer and stronger than our arms. As we walk or run, the bones in our feet and toes push against the ground, enabling us to move.

hip bones

thigh bone

calf bone

shin bone

ankle bones

foot bones

2. This mammal has long, slim legs. It can run very quickly to escape from predators.

3. The strong back legs of this mammal help it to leap away from danger. Its tail helps it to balance.

4. This mammal has four legs of the same size, so it is likely to walk or trot slowly.

What are muscles?

A skeleton cannot move on its own. It needs muscles to pull it in the right direction. Muscles are bundles of fibres which are made of overlapping threads of protein. Signals from a mammal's brain cause chemical reactions in the muscle fibres. These reactions make the threads in the fibres move closer together. This shortens the muscle and makes it move.

Most muscles are attached to a bone, and as the muscle contracts, it pulls the bone and the animal moves.

A typical mammal, such as a cat, has about 600 muscles. The labels on this diagram give the scientific names for some of the muscles.

trapezius

latissimus

biceps

vastus

gastrocnemius

digital extensors

triceps

Muscles in action

Muscles can pull hard, but they can't push, so most muscles work in pairs. One muscle contracts and pulls the bone one way, then its partner contracts to pull the bone back to its original position. Most movements involve several groups of muscles working together.

When a tiger runs, groups of muscles contract to pull its legs forwards and backwards.

Why do weightlifters have big muscles?

The more a muscle is used, the bigger and stronger it gets. Weightlifters do exercises to make their muscles bigger. But it is not necessary to have big bulging muscles for a body to work well.

What is cramp?

Cramp happens when a muscle suddenly contracts unexpectedly. This can happen if the muscle is strained during exercise, or if it is tensed unconsciously during sleep. Cramp can be very painful, and may last for several minutes before the muscle relaxes again.

How do mammals move?

A mammal's skeleton and muscle network are designed to help it to move in a particular way. Some mammals walk or run, others swim and others fly.

Orang-utans use their long arms and legs to swing through trees. They can grip on to branches using their hands and feet. Some monkeys have strong, muscular tails that they can use to hang from branches.

Mammals on land

Most mammals live on land, and get around by walking, running, jumping or swinging. Cheetahs can run very fast to catch their prey. Kangaroos can use their strong back legs to leap out of the way of danger.

Mammals in water

Mammals that live in seas and rivers have evolved bodies that help them to move through the water. Dolphins and whales have powerful muscles in their tails, which they swish up and down to move themselves forwards. Sea lions use their strong front flippers like wings to move swiftly through the water.

Otters have flaps of skin between their toes. As they swim, they spread their toes so that their webbed feet push against the water.

Mammals in the air

Bats are the only mammals that can fly. Their arms and hands have evolved to become wings, and they have strong muscles in their shoulders and chests to enable them to flap their wings. Bals vary greatly in size, from the tiny hog-nosed bat with a wingspan of 14cm to the huge flying fox with a body the size of a small dog and a wingspan of up to 2m.

finger bone

wrist

forearm bone

large flight muscles in chest and shoulders

upper-arm bone

tail bone

leg bones

wing

How fast can a human run compared to other mammals?

Many mammals could outrun the fastest Olympic sprinter. Animals need to be able to run fast in order to catch their prey or to escape from enemies.

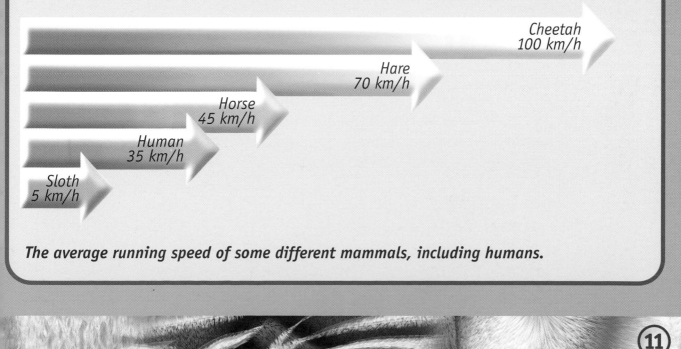

Cheetah
100 km/h

Hare
70 km/h

Horse
45 km/h

Human
35 km/h

Sloth
5 km/h

The average running speed of some different mammals, including humans.

Why do mammals eat?

Mammals need energy to survive. They need energy to hunt their prey or to run away from predators, and also to keep their blood at the right temperature. This energy is gained from food. Food also provides mammals with the nutrients they need to grow and to keep their bodies healthy.

From mouth to stomach

Most mammals chew their food before swallowing it. Chewing, together with saliva in the mouth, helps to break down the food into smaller pieces. The food is then swallowed, and passes along the gullet and into the stomach. In the stomach, the food is churned around and mixed with acidic juices until it becomes a thick liquid.

The intestines

This liquid then passes into the intestines. Here digestive juices break it down even further. Nutrients from the digested food pass into the blood, and are taken around the body. The body also stores some nutrients as fat. Mammals can draw on this fat for energy when there is a shortage of food. Any waste is stored at the end of the intestines, and passed from the body.

salivary glands which produce saliva

gullet

teeth

tongue

Do humans need to eat meat?

Mammals' bodies evolve to cope with the sort of food they eat. Some mammals, such as wolves and hyenas, are carnivorous, or meat-eating animals. Their digestive systems have developed in a way that enables their bodies to gain nutrients from meat. Other mammals, such as camels and elephants, are herbivores, or plant-eating animals. Their bodies have evolved in a different way to enable them to digest plants.

Humans are omnivores, which means we can digest a wide range of foods, including meat and many plants. Some people dislike the idea of eating meat, and become vegetarian. As long as a balanced diet is eaten, it is possible to survive whether or not meat is eaten.

small intestine

stomach

large intestine

The digestive system of a mammal.

Why do mammals breathe?

All mammals need to breathe. Even mammals that live underwater, such as whales and seals, need to come up for air. The air they breathe provides them with oxygen, which is needed for chemical reactions that maintain life. These reactions help a mammal's body to turn food into the energy it needs to grow, repair itself and maintain a constant temperature.

Most mammals breathe through their noses. The air then travels down the throat, into the windpipe and then into the lungs. The body parts used for breathing are called the respiratory system.

nose

throat

windpipe

lung

The respiratory system of a chamois.

How does the respiratory system work?

The bottom of the windpipe divides into two branches that go to the two lungs in the chest. These branches then divide again and again until they are about the width of a hair. At the end of these tiny tubes are bunches of microscopic air bubbles, called alveoli. The alveoli are surrounded by tiny blood vessels. These blood vessels pick up oxygen from the alveoli, so that this fresh supply of oxygen can be carried around the body in the mammal's blood.

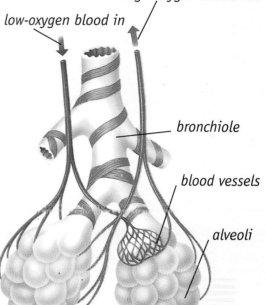

high-oxygen blood out

low-oxygen blood in

bronchiole

blood vessels

alveoli

What causes coughing?

As air is breathed in, tiny specks of dust and pollen are sucked into the throat along with the oxygen. Sometimes a speck gets stuck on the hairs that line the windpipe. Air needs to be forced through the windpipe to dislodge the speck. The brain tells the throat to close up, which means that pressure builds up in the lungs. This pressure forces air up the throat, taking the dust or pollen with it and making a loud coughing noise.

Why do I breathe faster when I exercise?

At rest, humans breathe in and out about fifteen times each minute. This increases to about 60 times each minute during exercise. This is because muscles are used more during exercise. The muscles need oxygen to work properly. So during exercise it is necessary to breathe faster in order to supply the muscles with the oxygen they need to keep working.

What does the **heart** do?

Every mammal has a heart. The heart is a pump that sends blood around the body, carrying the oxygen in the blood to areas where it is needed to make energy.

The heart is divided into two parts that do two different jobs. One part pumps blood to the lungs to pick up fresh supplies of oxygen, and the other part pumps this high-oxygen blood around the rest of the body.

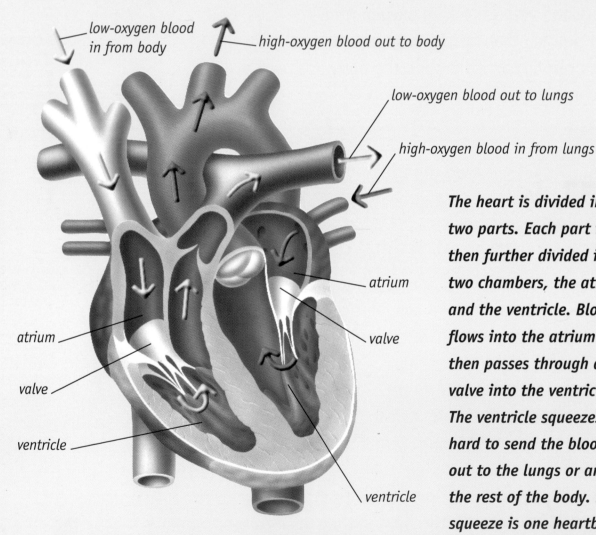

low-oxygen blood in from body

high-oxygen blood out to body

low-oxygen blood out to lungs

high-oxygen blood in from lungs

atrium

valve

atrium

valve

ventricle

ventricle

The heart is divided into two parts. Each part is then further divided into two chambers, the atrium and the ventricle. Blood flows into the atrium and then passes through a valve into the ventricle. The ventricle squeezes hard to send the blood out to the lungs or around the rest of the body. Each squeeze is one heartbeat.

warm blood

All mammals are warm-blooded. This means that a constant body temperature is maintained by the blood. When they are too hot, more blood is carried to the surface of the body, so that heat can escape through the skin. When they are too cold, less blood is pumped out to the surface of the body, so less heat is lost.

Why do I bleed?

Human blood is made up of liquid, called plasma, and solid pieces, called blood cells and platelets. When the skin is cut, the plasma flows out, carrying the blood cells and platelets with it. The blood is pushed out by the pumping of the heart.

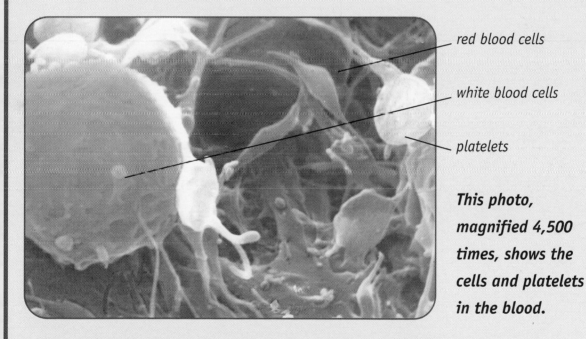

red blood cells

white blood cells

platelets

This photo, magnified 4,500 times, shows the cells and platelets in the blood.

How does the bleeding stop?

Soon after bleeding starts, some of the platelets in the blood join together. They produce tiny threads at the opening of the cut. These sticky threads form a net that traps the blood cells so that eventually the bleeding stops.

How does a mammal's brain work?

No one fully understands the way the brain works. However, scientists have discovered the functions of different areas of the brain.

*The **cerebrum** is by far the largest part of a mammal's brain. This section deals with the signals sent in from the senses, such as sights and smells. It also sends out signals to the muscles. The cerebrum is involved in many of the more complicated brain activities, such as making decisions.*

Why do I pull my hand away from something hot?

The human body contains millions of nerve cells. These cells pass messages around the body. The eyes pass messages to the nerve cells about things that are seen, the ears pass messages about things that are heard, the nose and tongue relay information about smells and tastes, and the skin detects touch and movement. When something hot is touched, nerves in the skin send lightning-fast messages along the nerve cells to the brain, warning it of danger. The brain sends back a message telling the muscles to move the hand away from the heat. This all happens in a fraction of a second, and is called a reflex action.

The **hypothalamus** is a small part at the front of the brain. It deals with basic feelings such as hunger and thirst.

The **cerebellum** is at the back of the brain. It controls the body's muscles and makes sure that complicated movements are carried out smoothly.

The **brain stem** is the lowest part of the brain. It controls basic body processes such as the heartbeat and breathing. These are activities that are carried out without consciously thinking about them.

How do mammals smell?

Mammals use their olfactory or smell organ to detect scents around them. Many mammals have a much more developed sense of smell than humans. They use their sense of smell to find food and to avoid predators and other dangers.

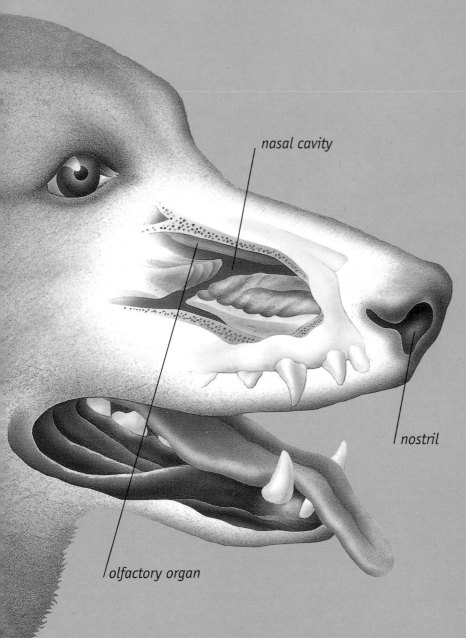

nasal cavity

nostril

olfactory organ

A mammal's nose

Inside a mammal's nose is an air-filled space called the nasal cavity. This space contains a patch of hairs, which is the olfactory organ. As air flows through the nasal cavity and across the hairs, nerve signals are sent to the brain, telling the mammal that there is an interesting smell around.

A dog's olfactory organ is more than 30 times bigger than that of a human. Dogs can detect smells thousands of times weaker than those humans can pick up.

Smelly signals

Many mammals use smells as signals. Antelopes and deer smear a strong-smelling liquid on to trees, as a warning to other deer to keep away from their territory. Skunks are famous for their ability to scare off enemies by squirting a foul-smelling liquid from under their tails.

The liquid squirted by a skunk not only smells disgusting, it also stings its enemy's eyes.

Why can't I smell things when I have a cold?

During a cold, a virus attacks the lining of the nose and throat, and the body makes extra mucus to protect itself. If your nose is filled with mucus, no air can reach the olfactory organ. Smell and taste are linked, which means it is also difficult to taste things.

How do mammals hear?

Mammals receive a great deal of information through their ears. Hearing helps them to pick up messages, to listen for predators and prey and to locate themselves within their environment.

Ear flaps

The visible part of the ear on the side of a mammal's head is called the ear flap. Different mammals have different shaped ear flaps. Rabbits and horses have large ear flaps, which makes their hearing very sensitive. Seals have tiny holes on the sides of their heads, because big ears would slow them down in the water. Many animals, such as dogs and deer, can move their ears to locate sounds.

Inside the ear

Most of a mammal's ear is actually inside its head. The ear flap leads into a short tunnel. At the end of this tunnel is the eardrum – a tiny piece of skin which vibrates when sounds hit it. These vibrations are then passed along tiny bones into the snail-shaped cochlea. The cochlea changes the vibrations into nerve signals, and sends these signals to the brain.

ear flap

skull bone

nerve to brain

cochlea

semicircular canals

eardrum

ear canal

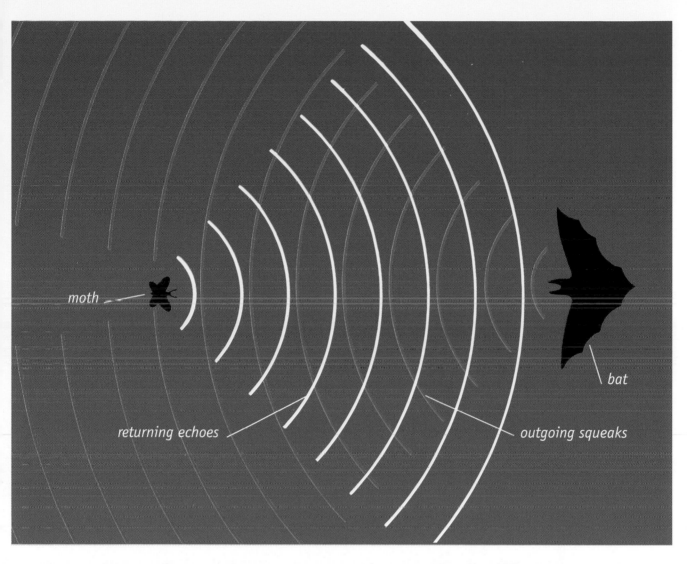

Bats use their excellent hearing to orientate themselves. The bat sends out tiny squeaks, then uses the echoes to locate objects such as moths. The bat can then swoop down on the moth in total darkness. This system is called echolocation.

Why do I get dizzy when I spin round?

The ears play an important part in helping to maintain balance. The three semicircular canals (see diagram) are filled with a liquid which moves as the body moves. The movement of the liquid sends messages to the brain about the position of the body. When you spin round, the liquid in the semicircular canals spins too. This confuses the brain, producing a feeling of dizziness.

How do mammals see?

All mammals have eyes that work in a similar way. They enable the animal to detect shapes, colours and movements, and they pass this information on to the brain.

Inside the eye

A mammal's eyes can adjust to allow it to see objects in bright and dim light, close up and far away. The pupil, the black spot in the centre of the eye, controls the amount of light entering the eye. It becomes smaller in bright light to protect the inside of the eye, then opens wide in dim light to let in as much light as possible. The lens, which is just behind the pupil, can adjust its shape to focus on near or far objects.

eye-moving muscles

eyelid
(closes to
protect eye)

lens

pupil

iris (controls size of pupil)

optic nerve (sends nerve
signals to brain)

Eye sizes

Different mammals' eyes have evolved to suit their lifestyle. Nocturnal animals, such as cats and bushbabies, have huge eyes to gather as much light as possible. Animals that live underground, such as moles, have tiny eyes, as they rely mainly on touch and hearing.

The African bushbaby uses its sharp sight and keen hearing to hunt at night.

Predators and prey

Mammals that are mainly hunters have eyes at the front of their heads. This helps them to focus clearly on the prey in front of them. Animals that are mainly the prey of other animals, such as deer and rabbits, have eyes on the sides of their head, so that they can see predators creeping up on them.

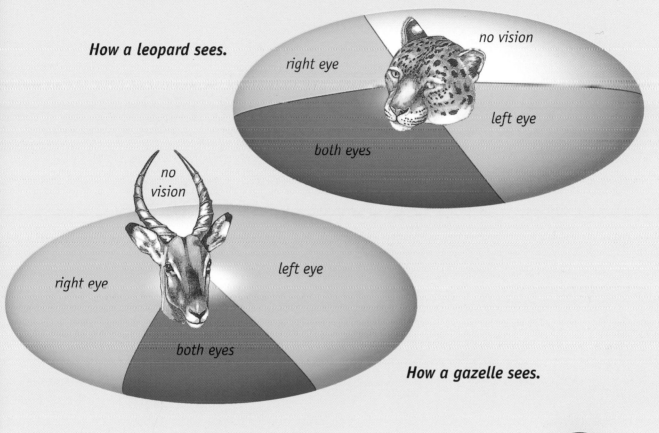

How a leopard sees.

no vision

right eye

left eye

both eyes

no vision

right eye

left eye

both eyes

How a gazelle sees.

Why do I blink?

The surface of the human eye has a thin layer of skin that is very sensitive to dust. With each blink, the eyelids wash over the surface of the eye with a liquid that cleans the dust away. Eyes are also protected by eyelids and eyelashes. If anything touches them, they send signals to the brain to close the eye to protect it.

How do mammals use camouflage?

Many mammals are able to camouflage themselves by blending into their surroundings. This makes it easier for them to hide from predators. For hunting animals, it can also make it easier for them to sneak up on their prey

Changing coats

Some mammals change the colour of their fur depending on the season. The Arctic hare, for example, has brown fur in the summer. This helps it to hide among leaves and dry grass. In the winter, it grows a thicker, white coat. This not only keeps it warm, but also means that it can now camouflage itself against the snow and ice.

Small animals such as this field vole are extremely vulnerable when feeding out in the open. If the vole keeps very still when it hears danger approaching, the predator may mistake it for a leaf and ignore it.

Spots, stripes and other patterns

Some mammals have patterned coats that act as camouflage. It might seem as if a badger's stripes make it stand out, but in the forest at night its coat looks just like patches of moonlight filtering through the trees. Other animals, such as zebras, have different coloured stripes that disguise their shape and make it difficult for predators to pick out one animal from the herd.

The ocelot's striped and spotted coat means that it is difficult to see it in the moonlight.

When I cut my hair, why doesn't it hurt?

Human hair and nails mostly consist of dead cells. They don't contain any nerves, so are unable to send any pain messages to the brain.

If hair is pulled, though, it does hurt! This is because there are nerve cells around the roots of the hair under the skin on your scalp. When the hair is pulled, these nerve cells send a message to the brain

How are mammals born?

Most mammals develop inside the mother's body. They live inside the mother's womb, and are supplied with food and oxygen by the placenta. After birth, the young are fed on the mother's milk.

This way of developing is unique to mammals. It gives the young animals a good chance of survival. Most mammals look after their young until they are ready to fend for themselves.

Marsupials

Some mammals develop in a slightly different way. Marsupials, such as kangaroos, only spend a short time in the mother's womb. A baby kangaroo is born naked, blind and unable to survive in the outside world, so it crawls into its mother's pouch for protection. Once inside the pouch, the baby kangaroo continues to grow and develop. As it becomes stronger, it is able to leave the pouch for short periods, and eventually it is ready to survive on its own.

A kangaroo with its young, or 'joey'.

Monotremes

Three mammals give birth in a completely different way. The platypus and two species of echidna are the only mammals that lay eggs. These mammals are called monotremes, which means 'egg-laying mammals'. When the eggs hatch, the young feed on their mother's milk, just like other mammals.

This platypus is guarding its nest.

Why do babies and children like to play?

Play, as well as being fun, also has a serious side. It enables children to practise the skills they will need later in life. Games that involve running around, jumping or playing with balls help to develop strong muscles and good muscle co-ordination. Playing with others teaches children to communicate clearly and to get along with other people.

Humans are not the only animals that play. Other young mammals also seem to play with each other. Baby chimps chase each other and have mock fights, kittens pounce on real and imaginary objects and chase balls, and puppies play tug of war with each other. These games help the young animals to prepare for life as adults.

Answers

Answers to 'Name the skeleton' on pages 6 and 7

1 sea lion

2 pronghorn

3 kangaroo

4 bear

Glossary

contract
to shorten

evolve
to change gradually from one generation to the next

mucus
a slimy substance produced by the lining of the nose and throat

muscle co-ordination
the ability to use several muscles together to make complicated movements

nutrient
a substance in food which helps animals and plants to grow and stay healthy

orientate
to find out where you are

predator
an animal that kills and eats other animals

prey
an animal killed by another animal for food

species
a group of animals or plants that have common characteristics
and can breed together

suckle
to feed a young animal on its mother's milk

vibrate
to move backwards and forwards very quickly

virus
a germ that can cause disease

vulnerable
weak; without protection

Index